War School for Dogs

Written by David
Illustrated by Robin

T0364586

Contents

Collins

Animals in war

For as long as countries have gone to war, animals have marched alongside the fighting men and women.

More than 3,000 years ago, an African general called Hannibal used elephants to attack the Romans. Horses have ridden into battle, pulled heavy **field guns** and carried supplies to the front. Dogs have long been used to carry top-secret messages, sniff out **explosives** and guard military bases. At other times, camels, dolphins, monkeys and even bats have been used in attempts to defeat an enemy.

Over the centuries, the number of animals used in wars has been enormous. An estimated eight million horses and **mules** died in the First World War alone, and thousands of soldiers, sailors and airmen from many different countries have adopted dogs, cats, goats, bears and at least one fox cub as **mascots**. Animals have helped keep the troops' spirits high, and as companions have served as a reminder of families and pets left behind at home.

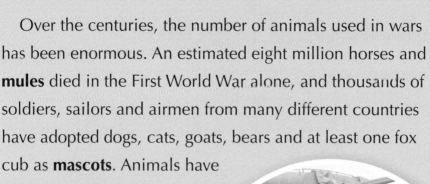

"Blackie", ship's cat on HMS *Prince of Wales*

3

1914: war is declared

Despite a long tradition of military animals, at the start of the First World War, the British army had just one trained dog. The German army had 6,000. This worried one army officer in particular.

Twenty years earlier, Lieutenant Colonel Edwin Richardson had noticed Germans buying English dogs for its army. Airedales, collies and sheepdogs were especially popular, and Richardson was concerned that in a future war these same animals could be used against British soldiers fighting in the **trenches**.

German soldiers
working with dogs

Richardson was a skilled dog trainer, and he knew how courageous, loyal and trustworthy they could be. He was convinced that dogs could be of great assistance to the army. With its speed and **stamina**, a good dog can run much faster than any man. Its sharp eyes and keen senses of smell and hearing could help defend Britain against its enemies.

Lieutenant Colonel Richardson

Training begins in Scotland

The government and the heads of the army didn't share Richardson's view. Hoping to change their minds, Richardson and his wife Blanche began training dogs themselves. The training took place at a farm they had bought at Carnoustie on the east coast of Scotland.

Blanche Richardson

To begin with, the plan was to supply trained animals to help the British Red Cross Society in its work treating the wounded. They hoped that seeing the dogs performing such a useful service might persuade the authorities to change their minds.

Airedales were a favourite **breed**. The Richardsons found them to be tough, energetic, physically strong and adaptable to any kind of climate. They were also loyal and highly intelligent, which the Richardsons admired.

Airedales being trained

7

British Red Cross dogs

Richardson trained his first Airedales to work as ambulance dogs, carrying first-aid supplies. He'd watched dogs working in Germany and Russia, and seen how good they were at finding injured soldiers on the battlefield. With its very good sense of hearing, a dog can detect the sound of someone breathing when a human can't. A dog's amazing sense of smell can help it find an **unconscious** soldier lying, injured and unseen, in an abandoned trench or shell hole.

The Richardsons demonstrated these skills at a nearby army **barracks**. The officers were impressed by the performance of two Airedales, Wolf and Prince, and several wrote to the **War Office** asking to have similar animals of their own.

Red Cross dogs were trained to bark when they found wounded soldiers.

8

Their requests were turned down. Even with
the knowledge that foreign armies were using more and
more dogs, the British army was still not ready to get
involved with something new and untried.

a man getting bandages
carried by a Red Cross dog

Wolf and Prince go off to war

As an experiment, Richardson sent Wolf and Prince to
the Western Front to serve with the British Red Cross.
The Western Front was the name given to the large area
of land where many of the First World War's biggest
battles took place and, as they delivered medical supplies,
Wolf and Prince faced the same dangers as ordinary soldiers.
Despite wearing bright British Red Cross symbols on their
sides, several ambulance dogs had already been shot at by
German **snipers**.

soldiers in a trench on
the Western Front

When he saw how well the dogs worked for the British Red Cross on the Western Front, Richardson decided to retrain them as messengers instead. Messenger dogs ran from trench to trench carrying important messages, rather than 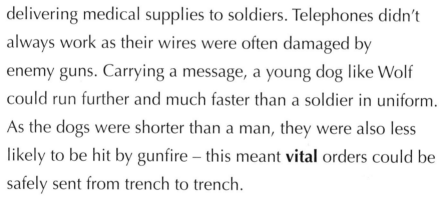 delivering medical supplies to soldiers. Telephones didn't always work as their wires were often damaged by enemy guns. Carrying a message, a young dog like Wolf could run further and much faster than a soldier in uniform. As the dogs were shorter than a man, they were also less likely to be hit by gunfire – this meant **vital** orders could be safely sent from trench to trench.

In 1916, after watching the dogs working over long distances, Colonel Winter of the Royal **Artillery** sent a report to London. He described how well the dogs had performed over rough and unfamiliar **terrain** and in very poor light. At last, those in charge in the army began to take notice.

The first British War Dog School

The following year, in 1917, the Richardsons were asked by the army to set up an official training school for military dogs at Shoeburyness in Essex. The facilities were much larger and more convenient than their farm in Scotland, and it was close to an **artillery range** so the dogs would get used to hearing weapons being fired.

The school's first recruits came from the Home for Lost Dogs at Battersea in London and were trained as message carriers. As new roles were found for these clever animals, more strays were brought from other dogs' homes and police **pounds** in Manchester, Birmingham, Liverpool and Bristol.

The sound of the guns was important. Richardson wanted to make the training as realistic as possible. He knew a dog trained in the peace and quiet of the countryside might be too scared to work when it encountered the noise and smoke and danger of the trenches.

Did you know?

The gunfire and explosions in France were so loud they could sometimes be heard as far away as London.

THE DOGS OF WAR: THE TRAINING OF CANINE DESPATCH-CARRIERS.

PHOTOGRAPHS BY SPORT AND GENERAL.

TRAINED TO FACE THE BULLETS: DOGS PASSING THROUGH A SQUAD OF SOLDIERS VOLLEY-FIRING.

THE WONDERFUL TRAINING OF MESSENGER-DOGS: PASSING UNDETERRED THROUGH A SMOKE-BARRAGE.

INSTRUCTIONS: A SIGNALLER PUTTING A DESPATCH IN A WALLET FASTENED TO THE DOG'S COLLAR.

ARRIVED AT HEADQUARTERS: A MAJOR RECEIVING THE DOG'S DESPATCH.

ON HIS WAY TO DELIVER THE DESPATCH: JUMPING A GATE.

TRAINED TO CLEAR ALL OBSTACLES IN TRAVELLING ACROSS COUNTRY: DOGS CROSSING A DITCH.

FASTER THAN ANY "RUNNER" IN CONVEYING DESPATCHES: DOGS JUMPING OVER BARBED WIRE.

The *London Illustrated News* ran a story about the dog school.

13

Calling for volunteers

The school needed a lot of dogs to train so the War Office placed advertisements in newspapers asking the public to send their own pets for military service. Thousands responded. Many did so out of a sense of **patriotism**, others because wartime **rationing** made it difficult to feed a large animal at home. They knew their beloved pets would be well looked after by the army.

All sorts of dogs began arriving at the school, top breeds as well as scruffy **mongrels**. Colonel Richardson was pleased to see them all and noted how even confused and homesick dogs soon settled down when they were greeted by kind human voices and excellent dinners.

Life at the school

Before long, the Richardsons had hundreds of dogs
at Shoeburyness. They were especially pleased each time
an Airedale arrived but, when testing new recruits for their
suitability, they soon discovered that most breeds could be
trained to perform well at something useful.

The key, Richardson
found, was a combination
of kindness, gentleness
and reward. The dogs
needed to behave well
and know how to follow
an instruction, but as a dog
lover himself Richardson
knew it was vital that they
enjoyed the training and
were generally happy with
their surroundings.

dog handlers with
the new recruits

No dogs were ever punished if they got something wrong. Any dog handler who was cross or impatient was sent away. So, too, was the odd dog who ate too much food or who proved too lazy to learn. Owners sometimes received a note thanking them and explaining the dog had turned out not to be suitable.

Simulating trench warfare

It took about five weeks to train a dog, and each day began the same way with a firing drill. This involved the staff firing guns. The guns fired blanks, not real bullets, but the noise must have been terrifying. Dogs were taught to run between the guns and to lie still. At other times, they would be taken up to the large field guns so that gradually they got used to the sound and smell of high explosive.

The animals were also trained to wear gas masks
(to protect them from the poisonous gases used in trench
warfare) and to navigate their way around the dangerous
terrain of the battlefield. The Richardsons hoped to reduce
the horrifying numbers of dead and wounded soldiers.
If their dogs could do some of the jobs being done by
soldiers, they knew it was possible to reduce the number of
casualties and save the lives of many soldiers.

dogs wearing specially
made gas masks

What did the dogs do?

Good communication is essential in battle so what the army needed at first was messenger dogs. When technology failed (as it often did) soldiers could use a pigeon to send a message in a tiny canister strapped to its leg. Birds were very fast and could cover huge distances, but not at night-time or in thick fog.

Wolf and Prince had already shown they could deliver messages too, using metal cylinders fixed to their collars. Covering several kilometres in just 15 minutes, the dogs could leap over barbed wire and find a safe, fast route through a waterlogged, shell-holed battlefield.

An officer watching one of the dogs working for the first time was amazed at its speed and the determined way it completed its task. Another dog managed to cover eight kilometres through thick mud in just 27 minutes. It would have taken a man more than two hours – and he might have been shot dead.

Did you know?

Pigeons are so good at delivering messages that, after navigating hundreds of kilometres at a time, several of them received medals for their valuable wartime service.

Streamlining the service

Soon an official army dog unit was established in northern France. Kennels were built near Étaples, a town far enough from the fighting to be safe but close enough that dogs could be sent quickly to wherever they were most needed.

Major Alec Waley was put in charge. He was an officer in the Royal Engineers who was **decorated** several times for bravery. Waley wasn't a dog trainer like the Richardsons, but he realised that, for the best results, the dogs should be in one place.

handlers with their dogs at Étaples

Before this, individual officers had to organise their own messenger service. Now, instead of being attached to different **regiments**, the dogs were looked after at the central kennels. They had their own handlers who accompanied them when they left Étaples.

rows of kennels

Training to be a dog handler

Training the right soldiers to handle the dogs took the same time as training a dog – five weeks. Many soldiers chosen as handlers were **gamekeepers** or shepherds before the war, or had worked looking after foxhounds in local hunts.

As soldiers, the men had to be fit and brave, but they also needed to have a sympathetic understanding of animals. Obeying orders was vital, but they also had to show **initiative** when making difficult decisions in the heat of battle.

dogs being trained in smoke-filled trenches

British messenger dogs with their handler

Above all, the Richardsons insisted that they must love dogs. The worst handlers were those who treated a dog as a kind of machine. The best realised that the most effective way to get a dog to perform well is through gentle persuasion rather than by punishment or threat.

Each dog was trained to return to its handler from an unknown position. It would be taken further away each time, gradually learning that the quicker it got back, the sooner it would get some food as a reward.

The front line

Teams of dogs and their soldier handlers were sent from Étaples to sectional kennels. These kennels were located behind the front line, close to those areas where the fighting was heaviest. Each sectional kennel was under the command of a sergeant and housed 48 dogs and 16 handlers. When dogs were needed to carry messages, three would be taken, together with a handler, to a position even closer to the fighting.

From there, the dogs would be collected by another soldier and taken down to the trenches. Messages were put in metal cylinders attached to the dogs' collars and the dogs then had to run alone, as fast as they could, through some of the most dangerous places along the Western Front. The handler waited for a dog to return and then took any message a dog had collected to the senior officer.

Did you know?

Messages carried by dogs described exactly what was happening at the Western Front. Others contained requests for supplies or **reinforcements**, or for more ammunition.

Sentries and guards

With fighting along a 640-kilometre line stretching from Switzerland to the North Sea, most of the dogs were sent to France or Belgium. Here millions of soldiers were fighting in the complex network of trenches that made up the Western Front. The challenges of communicating along such a long front were huge, and Britain and its **allies** eventually used more than 20,000 dogs.

The soldiers were astonished by the speed with which the dogs completed their missions. The handler responsible for a dog called Jim reported that "the journey he did used to take a man one hour and ten minutes to walk. Jim did it in 22 minutes, through barbed wire entanglements, and a large number of **batteries**." Dogs very rarely got lost, and even when soldiers tried to distract them, most of them had no difficulty finding their way back to the right trench.

a dog guarding a building with weapons in it

Some travelled even further and joined troops at Salonika in Greece. Trained as sentry dogs, these animals were sent to listening posts on the front line to warn of an approaching enemy. The dogs were taught not to bark, which would give away their position. They alerted their handlers to any potential danger with a low growl.

Others worked as guard dogs in Italy patrolling military supply depots. They were so good at this that the Richardsons received a letter from a grateful officer at the local base headquarters. In it, he said the dogs were doing the work of 16 men.

What else did dogs do in the First World War?

Sentry and guard duties were just two of the new roles taken on by dogs as the war dragged on. Depending on their size, strength and intelligence, the animals were soon working hard in lots of different ways.

Dogs called scouts had to be quiet and know how to follow instructions. Their job was to patrol ahead of a **platoon** of soldiers, sniffing out a concealed enemy position. By growling quietly or stiffening its tail, the dog could warn its handler of any danger before the troops came under attack.

Some of the animals were trained as casualty or mercy dogs. Like ambulance dogs, they were brilliant at finding injured soldiers and they carried a small pouch of first-aid equipment. They were also trained to stay with anyone who was dying, providing comfort and companionship to those men who couldn't be rescued. Smaller breeds, like Jack Russells and other terriers, were often kept in the trenches to kill rats and other vermin.

Dogs killed hundreds of rats in the trenches.

Wise faces and willing hearts

Richardson's description of his "students" shows his warm, caring personality. Though Airedales remained a favourite, he soon realised that different breeds had different skills that the army could use.

Doberman pinschers and German shepherds were intelligent and easily trained. A dark coat also meant that they could slip past an enemy without being seen. Lurchers made exceptionally good messengers because they were very fast and nimble.

Airedale terrier

Doberman pinscher

All the dogs could navigate obstacles more easily than a man. They were also better at coping with the effects of poisonous gases. But there were some dogs Richardson called his **"conscientious objectors"**. These weren't necessarily bad dogs, but for one reason or another they were too difficult to train. When this happened, the school couldn't keep them and so some dogs were sent back to the Home for Lost Dogs or returned to their owners.

Did you know?
A few breeds, such as fox terriers, were too playful and were more interested in having fun than working.

German shepherd

lurcher

Hero dogs: Joe, Lizzard, Whitefoot, Lloyd and Jack

Dogs were frequently mentioned in official army reports, and praised for their performance.

One handler, Private Davis, described how hard-working his dogs were once they got to France. Joe, he said, was as good in the night as he was in the day and "was worth his weight in gold". Lizzard could cover almost five kilometres in complete darkness in just 20 minutes. According to Davis, she could always be relied upon to deliver a message.

The three other dogs, an Airedale and two Welsh terriers, were looked after by their handler, Errington. Jack, Whitefoot and Lloyd had to find their way through many dangers, including traffic, stray dogs and terrified farm animals running scared from the shelling.

All three dogs were injured in gas attacks, and Jack sadly died, but together they saved many lives by delivering important messages and by avoiding the need for soldiers to risk their lives by running in the open.

Gibby the bulldog was the Canadian army's mascot. He was badly gassed but survived.

Dogs in foreign armies

With **canine** sentries and guards, Germany clearly led the way in using dogs, but by the end of the war, Britain had thousands of dogs performing many different tasks around Europe.

Other countries used them too. In France, dogs were used as pack animals, carrying small loads from one place to another as quickly as possible. The Italian army used them as sentries, particularly strong mountain breeds which had been used for herding sheep before the war.

the Belgian army used dogs to pull machine guns

Sweden and Holland had their own dog schools long before Shoeburyness opened, and some of Richardson's ideas were put into practice after he'd visited a similar school in Russia.

As allies, Canadian and Australian forces borrowed British dogs, and for a while only the Americans didn't want to use them. However, eventually they too began recruiting dogs, including one that became the most famous dog of the entire war.

an image of a Red Cross dog used to encourage Americans to enlist

EVEN A DOG ENLISTS WHY NOT YOU?

660 MARKET ST. SAN FRANCISCO
Or any U.S. Army Recruiting Station

America's hero dog: Sergeant Stubby

Stubby was a Boston or bull terrier, found wandering around a university in the USA. It wasn't clear who owned him, and when a group of soldiers finished training at the university, one of them **smuggled** him out and on to a **troopship** bound for France. By the time they arrived, Stubby had become the official mascot of the 102nd **Infantry** Regiment.

As a joke, Stubby was made a private, the lowest army rank, but he soon showed he could do more than just keep men company. During several battles, Stubby warned the soldiers about poison gas attacks – because he could smell the gas before they could – and found several wounded soldiers. Once Stubby even caught a German spy, and held on to the man's trousers in his jaws until help arrived.

For this last deed, he was "promoted", and as Sergeant Stubby, he went on to win more medals than any dog before or since.

Sergeant Stubby had a coat made for him with all his medals attached to it.

Recognising the heroes

Sergeant Stubby's achievements were often reported in American newspapers, and after the war, the *Aberdeen Evening Express* described for readers in Britain the huge contribution dogs had made.

Praising their former owners, the piece said:

... it is only fitting that they should know that their dogs have been the means of saving countless lives and much valuable property.

The skill, courage, and tenacity of those dogs has been amazing. During heavy **barrages**, when all other communications have been cut, the messenger dogs have made their way, and in many cases have brought messages of vital importance.

Sometimes they have been wounded in the performance of their duties, and there is a wonderful record of the determination with which wounded dogs have persisted in their duty ... Many a time a dog has brought a message in a few minutes over ground which would take a runner hours to cross.

The Second World War, 1939–1945

The success of the Richardsons' school ensured that military dogs continued to play an important role alongside British servicemen and women.

When a second war with Germany was declared, a new War Dogs Training School was planned. This opened in 1942, at Northaw in Middlesex, in what had been the headquarters of the Greyhound Racing Association.

Staff included professional dog trainers and vets, and four-legged recruits were quickly found with help from charities such as the **RSPCA** and the National Canine Defence League.

Richardson continued to train dogs during the Second World War.

Again, most of the dogs were volunteered by their owners, and as many as 7,000 were offered for service in the first two weeks. This time, many of the permanent staff were women, members of the Auxiliary Territorial Service or ATS. As uniformed "kennel maids", they were joined by soldiers sent from infantry regiments to be trained in canine warfare.

a kennel maid working at the new War Dogs Training School

Did you know?

Some staff had worked with dogs before the war, but others were nurses or office workers. At least one had been a ballet dancer.

43

Special training

The experience of the First World War meant training methods were well understood. Once again, some of the animals went on to carry messages, but others were trained for patrol and guard duty.

For the first time, some of the school's 3,300 dogs were used as **mine** detectors. This very dangerous task relied on the dogs' **superior** sense of smell and an ability to remain calm and focused in the heat of battle.

Dogs can be trained to identify the smell of the explosives in a mine.

Rex was a black Labrador who had come to Northaw as a stray. In 1945, working in Germany's Reichswald Forest, he found so many mines that his platoon commander, Lieutenant Peter Norbury, called him the bravest dog he'd ever seen. Without Rex's dedication to duty, Norbury insisted, many men would have been injured or even died. At least 200 of the school's dogs never came home. Many were killed in action or were lost in the confusion of war.

Did you know?

Today, there are over 900 mine detection dogs working around the world.

allied soldiers advancing in the Reichswald Forest

Hero dog: Brian the paradog

Among the most dangerous and extraordinary missions of the Second World War were those involving animals travelling deep into enemy territory. Some dogs accompanied soldiers; others went with spies. More than a few found themselves behind enemy lines when aircraft they were travelling in were shot down by enemy guns.

Perhaps the most remarkable were the so-called "paradogs". One called Rob made 20 parachute jumps with British Special Forces serving in North Africa. Another, a German shepherd-collie cross called Brian, was parachuted into France as part of the **D-Day landings**. He landed in a tree, was shot at by a German sniper, and later injured by **mortar fire**. Despite this, he went on to perform a variety of guard and sniffer-dog duties. After the war, Brian went back to his family in Nottingham.

Dogs were parachuted behind enemy lines.

Military dogs today

Many dogs died in both world wars, but now trainers do everything possible to minimise the dangers they face.

Today, the responsibility for this lies with the 1st Military Working Dog Regiment, a unit made up of around 300 soldiers and nearly 400 dogs. These dogs have been involved in conflicts in Northern Ireland, the Balkans, Iraq and Afghanistan, and have travelled as far afield as Australia and Pakistan on other operations.

soldiers from the 1st Military Working Dog Regiment with their dogs

In the past, official army regulations warned handlers not to make friends with their dogs or to pet them, but today handlers and their dogs form a strong and close relationship.

Their work together is stressful and highly dangerous, and missions are not always successful. When trying to locate and **diffuse** explosive devices or home-made bombs, both dogs and humans have been injured or killed. Dogs fitted with video cameras have also come under attack after being sent into dangerous buildings looking for terrorists.

a military working dog wearing a camera and a protective helmet

The PDSA Dickin Medal

Brian the paradog was one of the first dogs to be awarded the Dickin Medal. This is the animal equivalent of the Victoria Cross, the very highest award for bravery.

In nearly three-quarters of a century, only 68 animals have received the medal. Horses, pigeons and even a cat called Simon have been honoured – as well as dogs.

The medal was the idea of Maria Dickin. As founder of the People's Dispensary for Sick Animals charity, she wanted to reward acts of extraordinary courage and loyalty in wartime. Since 1943, it has been given to animals that have saved lives in the most extreme circumstances, often at the cost of their own.

Lucca, a retired US Marine Corps dog, receiving her PDSA Dickin Medal

Their stories are fascinating and moving, and often very sad. Like those first Airedales trained by Lieutenant Colonel Richardson and his wife, they performed a valuable service and one we should be grateful for. They show us a dog really can be man's best friend and – more importantly – that not all heroes are human.

Glossary

allies   countries which agree to fight on the same side in a war

artillery   big guns used to destroy enemy trenches before an attack by troops

artillery range   a large stretch of open countryside where soldiers learn how to fire big guns accurately

barracks   a building where soldiers live and work

barrages   attacks on the enemy made by firing many big guns at the same time

batteries   groups of big guns firing in unison at the enemy

breed   type (of animal)

canine   a word that means "dog"

casualties   soldiers killed, wounded or missing after a battle

conscientious objectors   a name given to those who refuse to perform military service

decorated   given a medal as a reward for doing something brave

D-Day landings   the name given to the Allied invasion of Europe, freeing it from German occupation in 1945

diffuse   make an explosive device safe

explosives   a substance put in bombs or shells that is made to explode

field guns   large front-line weapons

gamekeepers   people who look after wild animals and birds that are kept for hunting

infantry   soldiers who go into battle on foot

initiative   ability to make a new plan if a situation changes

mascots   animals adopted by a military unit for ceremonial purposes

mine   explosives hidden underground to kill or injure troops

mongrels   dogs whose parents are different breeds

mortar fire   ammunition fired from a large gun

mules   animals which are a cross between a horse and a donkey, used for carrying supplies

patriotism   the good feeling a person has about his or her country

platoon   a small group of soldiers, around 15–30 in number

pounds   places where stray dogs are kept after being caught or rescued

rationing   a way of ensuring food is fairly shared in times of shortages

regiments	large units of soldiers, from a few hundred to a couple of thousand
reinforcements	extra troops who arrive to help
RSPCA	the Royal Society for the Prevention of Cruelty to Animals
smuggled	took something to or from a place illegally
snipers	concealed soldiers employed to shoot at the enemy
stamina	the ability to work long and hard at a demanding task
superior	better than
terrain	landscape, area
trenches	over 640 kilometres of dug-out earth where soldiers lived and fought
troopship	a ship used to transport large numbers of soldiers
unconscious	someone who is not conscious/awake as a result of an injury
vital	essential
War Office	the government ministry in charge of the army, navy and air force

Index

Man's best friend

Red Cross ambulance dog

messenger dog

mascot dog

paradog

sentry and guard dog

mine detector dog

Ideas for reading

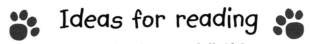

Written by Clare Dowdall, PhD
Lecturer and Primary Literacy Consultant

Reading objectives:
- make comparisons within and across books
- draw inferences and justify these with evidence
- retrieve, record and present information from non-fiction

Spoken language objectives:
- articulate and justify answers, arguments and opinions

Curriculum links: History – British history beyond 1066

Resources: pens and paper; ICT for research.

Build a context for reading

- Look closely at the front cover and ask children to describe what they can see happening.
- Read the title. Ask children what *War School for Dogs* is, and what they think the dog has learned to do there.
- Read the blurb aloud. Discuss what children know about the First World War and check that they know what a trench is. Ask children to infer why dogs were used to carry messages along them.

Understand and apply reading strategies

- Read through the contents together. Ask children what they can infer and deduce about how dogs were used in wartime from the contents.
- Turn to pp2–3. Read the text and then challenge children to recount how animals have been used in times of war.
- Pose the question *How can dogs help to win wars?* Using the text on pp4-5, model how to skim to find some ideas that answer the question quickly and efficiently.